AFTER THE KILL

Darrin Lunde

Illustrated by **Catherine Stock**

ﾭ Charlesbridge

For Sakura, Asahi, and Midori—
three little scavengers at my table
—D. L.

For Tarquin
—C. S.

Published by Charlesbridge
85 Main Street
Watertown, MA 02472
(617) 926-0329
www.charlesbridge.com

Library of Congress Cataloging-in-Publication Data
Lunde, Darrin P.
    After the kill / Darrin Lunde; illustrated by Catherine Stock.
        p. cm.
      ISBN 978-1-57091-743-1 (reinforced hardcover)
      ISBN 978-1-57091-744-8 (softcover)
1. Animals—Food—Juvenile literature. 2. Food chains
(Ecology)—Juvenile literature. I. Stock, Catherine, ill. II. Title.
QL756.5.L86 2011
591.5'3—dc22   2010007524
Printed in Singapore
(hc) 10 9 8 7 6 5 4 3 2 1
(sc) 10 9 8 7 6 5 4 3 2 1

Illustrations done in pencil, watercolor, and gouache
Display type set in Rakugaki, text type set in Sabon,
    and caption type set in Palatino Sans Informal
Color separations by Chroma Graphics, Singapore
Printed and bound February 2011 by Imago in Singapore
Production supervision by Brian G. Walker
Designed by Susan Mallory Sherman

It is early in the morning, and a hungry lioness is on the prowl. She sees a herd of zebras grazing in the distance. Mmmm—zebra! Her mouth begins to water.

The lioness crouches in the grass and creeps forward.

One of the zebras seems weaker than the others, and she focuses on it. The zebra twitches its ears, but it does not see her. The lioness creeps closer . . . closer . . . and then—

She springs from the grass, chases down the zebra, claws it in the back, pulls it to the ground, and bites it in the throat.

The zebra is dead. The lioness has killed it.

The Serengeti Plain of East Africa is home to some of the largest concentrations of animals on earth. Vast herds of wildebeests, zebras, and antelopes thrive on the plain, as do the predators and scavengers that feed on them.

After the kill, the lioness rips the carcass open and feasts on the soft internal organs first. Her sisters watch from across the plain and slowly walk toward her. The lionesses belong to the same pride and share their food.

Lions are social animals that live in groups called prides. Males and females play very different roles: females do most of the hunting, while males protect the pride. When a female kills an animal, the males usually—but not always—eat first.

While the lionesses are feeding, a white-backed vulture swoops in at high speed. *Thump!* It lands near the kill and spreads its wings wide. It hisses threateningly, kicks its feet, and rushes in closer. More vultures follow, and soon the carcass is swarming. The vultures reach deep inside the dead zebra with their long necks and tear off bits of meat and intestine.

White-backed vultures are such clumsy fliers that they sometimes crash-land near a kill with a forward somersault. They have hooked tongues that keep other vultures from snatching slippery meat out of their mouths.

A wandering spotted hyena sees the vultures and trots up to the kill. It is afraid of the lionesses and circles at a safe distance. Other members of the hyena clan join it. *Ooo, ooo! Whoop, whoop! Hee, hee, hee!* They grunt, whoop, and laugh as they slowly circle closer. A single hyena is no match for a lion, but a group of hyenas is strong. It is time for the lionesses to leave.

Hyenas are very well adapted as scavengers, but they also hunt their own food. Sometimes a lion will scavenge food from hyenas.

The hyenas devour the zebra in a frenzy of biting and pulling. They tear entire limbs and large pieces of meat from the carcass, making eerie laughing sounds as they squabble. They can eat every part of the carcass, including the skin and bones.

Hyenas have specialized teeth for slicing tough skin and crushing hard bone. Their long canines help them grip and pull slippery meat.

One of the hyenas has dragged away a piece of the zebra's neck and is crunching on it. Two golden jackals approach the hyena from opposite sides until they are right beside it. The angry hyena snaps its teeth at the jackal to its left, while the jackal to its right quickly snatches the meat and runs away.

This technique, in which pairs of jackals approach a hyena from opposite sides to steal food, is called yo-yoing. Hyenas will kill and eat jackals if they can catch them, but jackals are quick and almost always escape.

The fleeing jackal and pursuing hyena race past three big male lions sleeping in the morning sunshine. The largest wakes up and notices the clan of hyenas feasting on the zebra carcass. He is hungry after his nap. He raises the hairs of his mane and opens his mouth wide.

ROAR!

Lions and hyenas are enemies because they compete for the same food. While a clan of hyenas can drive female lions from their kill, a big male lion can stand them down.

Female spotted hyenas are bigger than males,
and the female leading the clan is often one of
the largest.

He races to the kill, charges the clan, chases the largest female, and swipes her with his claws. The hyenas flee in terror. Once again the carcass belongs to the pride.

The three big males settle down in front of the kill and chew large pieces of meat from the legs. Several small lion cubs join them. They tear into the carcass and play tug-of-war with scraps of meat.

A lioness hides her cubs in a safe place before she sets out on a hunt. After she has had a chance to eat, she brings her cubs to the kill. She carries them in her teeth by the loose skin of their necks.

Their bellies full at last, the lions wander away from the carcass and roll onto their backs to rest. Dozens more white-backed vultures descend on the kill. They push and shove and stand on each other's backs as they fight ferociously for the remaining pieces of meat. Tiny bits of muscle and guts are tossed into the air and picked up by hooded vultures roaming the perimeter for scraps.

Hooded vultures are small, agile fliers that usually have no trouble avoiding larger predators. If a lion gets close enough to swat one with his paws, the vulture will play dead until the lion loses interest.

A pair of huge lappet-faced vultures glides in and slowly spirals down beside the kill. The white-backed and hooded vultures continue fighting over food until one of the lappet-faced vultures spreads its wings, opens its mouth, and thrusts its head forward as it rushes in to attack. *Flap, flap, flap, flap, flap!* The other vultures fly away, leaving nothing behind but fluttering feathers. The two lappet-faced vultures eat in peace.

Lappet-faced vultures are also called king vultures. They eat the tough skin and connective tissue that no other vulture can eat.

The skeleton is still covered with little bits of flesh. Crawling up from the ground, thousands of tiny meat-eating beetles swarm inside the skull, squeeze between the teeth, and wiggle inside the ears. They pick at the zebra bones until at last the skeleton is clean.

Meat-eating beetles belong to a family of beetles called dermestids. Dermestid beetles are so good at cleaning skeletons that most natural history museums keep living colonies of them for cleaning their skeletons.

The smooth bones shine white under the setting
African sun. They will lie there on the Serengeti Plain
until they slowly turn to dust.